WHALE

ADDRESS

BOOK

&

TRIVIA

A design by Pamela Garcia
Star Dust Dreams Publishing

Names & Addresses

Record the names, addresses and a few words

about family and friends.

Name _____

Address _____ Apt/Unit # _____

City _____ State _____ Zip _____

Phone _____ Cell_____

E-mail _____

Notes _____

_____

_____

Name _____

Address _____ Apt/Unit # _____

City _____ State _____ Zip _____

Phone _____ Cell_____

E-mail _____

Notes _____

_____

_____

Name _____

Address _____ Apt/Unit # _____

City _____ State _____ Zip _____

Phone _____ Cell_____

E-mail _____

Notes _____

_____

_____

Name _____

Address _____ Apt/Unit # _____

City _____ State _____ Zip _____

Phone _____ Cell_____

E-mail _____

Notes _____

_____

═══

Name _____

Address _____ Apt/Unit # _____

City _____ State _____ Zip _____

Phone _____ Cell_____

E-mail _____

Notes _____

_____

═══

Name _____

Address _____ Apt/Unit # _____

City _____ State _____ Zip _____

Phone _____ Cell_____

E-mail _____

Notes _____

_____

═══

Name _____

Address _____ Apt/Unit # _____

City _____ State _____ Zip _____

Phone _____ Cell_____

E-mail _____

Notes _____

_____

═══

Name _____

Address _____ Apt/Unit # _____

City _____ State _____ Zip _____

Phone _____ Cell_____

E-mail _____

Notes _____

_____

═══

Name _____

Address _____ Apt/Unit # _____

City _____ State _____ Zip _____

Phone _____ Cell_____

E-mail _____

Notes _____

_____

═══

Name _____

Address _____ Apt/Unit # _____

City _____ State _____ Zip _____

Phone _____ Cell_____

E-mail _____

Notes _____

_____

===

Name _____

Address _____ Apt/Unit # _____

City _____ State _____ Zip _____

Phone _____ Cell_____

E-mail _____

Notes _____

_____

===

Name _____

Address _____ Apt/Unit # _____

City _____ State _____ Zip _____

Phone _____ Cell_____

E-mail _____

Notes _____

_____

===

Name _____

Address _____ Apt/Unit # _____

City _____ State _____ Zip _____

Phone _____ Cell_____

E-mail _____

Notes _____

_____

═══

Name _____

Address _____ Apt/Unit # _____

City _____ State _____ Zip _____

Phone _____ Cell_____

E-mail _____

Notes _____

_____

═══

Name _____

Address _____ Apt/Unit # _____

City _____ State _____ Zip _____

Phone _____ Cell_____

E-mail _____

Notes _____

_____

_____

Name _____

Address _____ Apt/Unit # _____

City _____ State _____ Zip _____

Phone _____ Cell_____

E-mail _____

Notes _____

_____

═══

Name _____

Address _____ Apt/Unit # _____

City _____ State _____ Zip _____

Phone _____ Cell_____

E-mail _____

Notes _____

_____

═══

Name _____

Address _____ Apt/Unit # _____

City _____ State _____ Zip _____

Phone _____ Cell_____

E-mail _____

Notes _____

_____

═══

Name _____

Address _____ Apt/Unit # _____

City _____ State _____ Zip _____

Phone _____ Cell_____

E-mail _____

Notes _____

_____

═══

Name _____

Address _____ Apt/Unit # _____

City _____ State _____ Zip _____

Phone _____ Cell_____

E-mail _____

Notes _____

_____

═══

Name _____

Address _____ Apt/Unit # _____

City _____ State _____ Zip _____

Phone _____ Cell_____

E-mail _____

Notes _____

_____

_____

Name _____

Address _____ Apt/Unit # _____

City _____ State _____ Zip _____

Phone _____ Cell_____

E-mail _____

Notes _____

_____

_____

Name _____

Address _____ Apt/Unit # _____

City _____ State _____ Zip _____

Phone _____ Cell_____

E-mail _____

Notes _____

_____

_____

Name _____

Address _____ Apt/Unit # _____

City _____ State _____ Zip _____

Phone _____ Cell_____

E-mail _____

Notes _____

_____

_____

Name _____

Address _____ Apt/Unit # _____

City _____ State _____ Zip _____

Phone _____ Cell_____

E-mail _____

Notes _____

_____

===

Name _____

Address _____ Apt/Unit # _____

City _____ State _____ Zip _____

Phone _____ Cell_____

E-mail _____

Notes _____

_____

===

Name _____

Address _____ Apt/Unit # _____

City _____ State _____ Zip _____

Phone _____ Cell_____

E-mail _____

Notes _____

_____

_____

Name _____

Address _____ Apt/Unit # _____

City _____ State _____ Zip _____

Phone _____ Cell_____

E-mail _____

Notes _____

_____

═══

Name _____

Address _____ Apt/Unit # _____

City _____ State _____ Zip _____

Phone _____ Cell_____

E-mail _____

Notes _____

_____

═══

Name _____

Address _____ Apt/Unit # _____

City _____ State _____ Zip _____

Phone _____ Cell_____

E-mail _____

Notes _____

_____

_____

Whale Trivia

(Answers are in the back of the book)

1. How many nostrils does a toothed whale have?

      ___ One   ___ Two

      ___ Three   ___ Whales don't have nostrils

2. What is baleen like?

      ___ Our hair   ___ Our fingernails

      ___ Our toe nails   ___ All the above

3. How many chambers does a whale's heart have?

      ___ Two   ___ Three

      ___ Six   ___ Four

4. What is the largest animal to have ever lived?

      ___ Elephant   ___ Blue whale

      ___ Dinosaur   ___ Megalodon

5. Which whale has the longest migration?

      ___ Gray whale   ___ Humpback whale

      ___ Sei whale   ___ Blue whale

6. Do whales have hind limbs (legs)?

      ___ Yes   ___ No

7. Where do deep diving whales store their oxygen?

      ___ Lungs   ___ Muscles

      ___ Nose   ___ Melon

8. All whales locate food by sonar or echolocation.

      ___ True   ___ False

Name _____

Address _____ Apt/Unit # _____

City _____ State _____ Zip _____

Phone _____ Cell_____

E-mail _____

Notes _____

_____

══

Name _____

Address _____ Apt/Unit # _____

City _____ State _____ Zip _____

Phone _____ Cell_____

E-mail _____

Notes _____

_____

══

Name _____

Address _____ Apt/Unit # _____

City _____ State _____ Zip _____

Phone _____ Cell_____

E-mail _____

Notes _____

_____

_____

Name _____

Address _____ Apt/Unit # _____

City _____ State _____ Zip _____

Phone _____ Cell_____

E-mail _____

Notes _____

_____

Name _____

Address _____ Apt/Unit # _____

City _____ State _____ Zip _____

Phone _____ Cell_____

E-mail _____

Notes _____

_____

Name _____

Address _____ Apt/Unit # _____

City _____ State _____ Zip _____

Phone _____ Cell_____

E-mail _____

Notes _____

_____

_____

Name _____

Address _____ Apt/Unit # _____

City _____ State _____ Zip _____

Phone _____ Cell _____

E-mail _____

Notes _____

_____

==

Name _____

Address _____ Apt/Unit # _____

City _____ State _____ Zip _____

Phone _____ Cell _____

E-mail _____

Notes _____

_____

==

Name _____

Address _____ Apt/Unit # _____

City _____ State _____ Zip _____

Phone _____ Cell _____

E-mail _____

Notes _____

_____

_____

Name _____

Address _____ Apt/Unit # _____

City _____ State _____ Zip _____

Phone _____ Cell_____

E-mail _____

Notes _____

_____

Name _____

Address _____ Apt/Unit # _____

City _____ State _____ Zip _____

Phone _____ Cell_____

E-mail _____

Notes _____

_____

Name _____

Address _____ Apt/Unit # _____

City _____ State _____ Zip _____

Phone _____ Cell_____

E-mail _____

Notes _____

_____

_____

Name _____

Address _____ Apt/Unit # _____

City _____ State _____ Zip _____

Phone _____ Cell_____

E-mail _____

Notes _____

_____

===

Name _____

Address _____ Apt/Unit # _____

City _____ State _____ Zip _____

Phone _____ Cell_____

E-mail _____

Notes _____

_____

===

Name _____

Address _____ Apt/Unit # _____

City _____ State _____ Zip _____

Phone _____ Cell_____

E-mail _____

Notes _____

_____

_____

Name _____

Address _____ Apt/Unit # _____

City _____ State _____ Zip _____

Phone _____ Cell _____

E-mail _____

Notes _____

_____

Name _____

Address _____ Apt/Unit # _____

City _____ State _____ Zip _____

Phone _____ Cell _____

E-mail _____

Notes _____

_____

Name _____

Address _____ Apt/Unit # _____

City _____ State _____ Zip _____

Phone _____ Cell _____

E-mail _____

Notes _____

_____

Name _____

Address _____ Apt/Unit # _____

City _____ State _____ Zip _____

Phone _____ Cell_____

E-mail _____

Notes _____

_____

Name _____

Address _____ Apt/Unit # _____

City _____ State _____ Zip _____

Phone _____ Cell_____

E-mail _____

Notes _____

_____

Name _____

Address _____ Apt/Unit # _____

City _____ State _____ Zip _____

Phone _____ Cell_____

E-mail _____

Notes _____

_____

TOOTHED & NON-TOOTHED WHALES

Whales are grouped into eight families: The right whale (Balaenidae), pygmy right whale (Cetotheriidae), the gray whale (Escrichtiidae), the belugas and narwhals (Monodontidae), the rorquals (Balaenopteridae), the sperm whale (Physeteridae), the dwarf and pygmy sperm whale (Kogiidae) and the beaked whales (Ziphiidae).

Whales are divided into two groups:

Toothed whales (Odontocetes) – have conical teeth and one blow hole. They locate their prey by echolocation. They range in size from 4.5 ft and 120 lbs. to 66 ft. and 55 tons). The majority of toothed whales eat fish and squid, but some orcas also eat sea mammals such as seals, sea lions, penguins and other whales.

Baleen whale (Mysticetes) – have plates of sieve-like structures across the top of their mouth made of keratin (the same thing our fingernails and hair are made of) and two blow holes. The baleen can range from inches to 15 ft. Baleen whales are the largest of the whale species, ranging from 20 ft to 110 ft. and 6,600 lb. to 150 ton. Since they have no teeth, baleen whales normally feed on krill, plankton, shrimp, small fish and other cetaceans. The take in large mouthfuls of water filled with prey, then push out the water through the baleen, leaving the food inside. The family rorquals have throat pleats that extend from their chins to their navels. These pleats expand, allowing the whale to take in larger mouthfuls of water and food. The baleen has often been compared to the teeth in a comb.

Name _____

Address _____ Apt/Unit # _____

City _____ State _____ Zip _____

Phone _____ Cell_____

E-mail _____

Notes _____

_____

Name _____

Address _____ Apt/Unit # _____

City _____ State _____ Zip _____

Phone _____ Cell_____

E-mail _____

Notes _____

_____

Name _____

Address _____ Apt/Unit # _____

City _____ State _____ Zip _____

Phone _____ Cell_____

E-mail _____

Notes _____

_____

_____

Name _____

Address _____ Apt/Unit # _____

City _____ State _____ Zip _____

Phone _____ Cell _____

E-mail _____

Notes _____

_____

Name _____

Address _____ Apt/Unit # _____

City _____ State _____ Zip _____

Phone _____ Cell _____

E-mail _____

Notes _____

_____

Name _____

Address _____ Apt/Unit # _____

City _____ State _____ Zip _____

Phone _____ Cell _____

E-mail _____

Notes _____

_____

_____

Name _____

Address _____ Apt/Unit # _____

City _____ State _____ Zip _____

Phone _____ Cell_____

E-mail _____

Notes _____

_____

Name _____

Address _____ Apt/Unit # _____

City _____ State _____ Zip _____

Phone _____ Cell_____

E-mail _____

Notes _____

_____

Name _____

Address _____ Apt/Unit # _____

City _____ State _____ Zip _____

Phone _____ Cell_____

E-mail _____

Notes _____

_____

_____

Name _____

Address _____ Apt/Unit # _____

City _____ State _____ Zip _____

Phone _____ Cell_____

E-mail _____

Notes _____

_____

Name _____

Address _____ Apt/Unit # _____

City _____ State _____ Zip _____

Phone _____ Cell_____

E-mail _____

Notes _____

_____

Name _____

Address _____ Apt/Unit # _____

City _____ State _____ Zip _____

Phone _____ Cell_____

E-mail _____

Notes _____

_____

_____

Name _____

Address _____ Apt/Unit # _____

City _____ State _____ Zip _____

Phone _____ Cell_____

E-mail _____

Notes _____

_____

Name _____

Address _____ Apt/Unit # _____

City _____ State _____ Zip _____

Phone _____ Cell_____

E-mail _____

Notes _____

_____

Name _____

Address _____ Apt/Unit # _____

City _____ State _____ Zip _____

Phone _____ Cell_____

E-mail _____

Notes _____

_____

_____

Name _____

Address _____ Apt/Unit # _____

City _____ State _____ Zip _____

Phone _____ Cell_____

E-mail _____

Notes _____

_____

Name _____

Address _____ Apt/Unit # _____

City _____ State _____ Zip _____

Phone _____ Cell_____

E-mail _____

Notes _____

_____

Name _____

Address _____ Apt/Unit # _____

City _____ State _____ Zip _____

Phone _____ Cell_____

E-mail _____

Notes _____

_____

Name _____

Address _____ Apt/Unit # _____

City _____ State _____ Zip _____

Phone _____ Cell_____

E-mail _____

Notes _____

_____

Name _____

Address _____ Apt/Unit # _____

City _____ State _____ Zip _____

Phone _____ Cell_____

E-mail _____

Notes _____

_____

Name _____

Address _____ Apt/Unit # _____

City _____ State _____ Zip _____

Phone _____ Cell_____

E-mail _____

Notes _____

_____

Whale Trivia

9. Do whales have ears?

    ___ Yes   ___ No

10. All dolphins are whales.

    ___ True   ___ False

11. Which toothed whale also eats marine mammals?

    ___ Sperm Whale   ___ Fin Whale

    ___ Orca   ___ Blue Whale

12. What is a whale?

    ___ A fish   ___ A mammal

    ___ An amphibian   ___ A reptile

13. The ancestor of the whales was a land creature who walked on all four leg.

    ___ True   ___ False

14. What was the nick name given to Gray whales by whalers?

    ___ Scourge of the Sea   ___ Devil Fish

    ___ Easy Prey   ___ Puddle Jumpers

15. How large is a blue whale's heart?

    ___ The size of a Volkswagen Beetle car

    ___ Weighs about 1300 lbs.

    ___ Can be heard from two miles away

    ___ A two-year old child can crawl through the aorta

    ___ All the above

16. A porpoise and a dolphin are the same mammal?

    ___ True   ___ False

Name _____

Address _____ Apt/Unit # _____

City _____ State _____ Zip _____

Phone _____ Cell_____

E-mail _____

Notes _____

_____

Name _____

Address _____ Apt/Unit # _____

City _____ State _____ Zip _____

Phone _____ Cell_____

E-mail _____

Notes _____

_____

Name _____

Address _____ Apt/Unit # _____

City _____ State _____ Zip _____

Phone _____ Cell_____

E-mail _____

Notes _____

_____

Name _____

Address _____ Apt/Unit # _____

City _____ State _____ Zip _____

Phone _____ Cell_____

E-mail _____

Notes _____

_____

Name _____

Address _____ Apt/Unit # _____

City _____ State _____ Zip _____

Phone _____ Cell_____

E-mail _____

Notes _____

_____

Name _____

Address _____ Apt/Unit # _____

City _____ State _____ Zip _____

Phone _____ Cell_____

E-mail _____

Notes _____

_____

_____

Name _____

Address _____ Apt/Unit # _____

City _____ State _____ Zip _____

Phone _____ Cell_____

E-mail _____

Notes _____

_____

===

Name _____

Address _____ Apt/Unit # _____

City _____ State _____ Zip _____

Phone _____ Cell_____

E-mail _____

Notes _____

_____

===

Name _____

Address _____ Apt/Unit # _____

City _____ State _____ Zip _____

Phone _____ Cell_____

E-mail _____

Notes _____

_____

_____

Name _____

Address _____ Apt/Unit # _____

City _____ State _____ Zip _____

Phone _____ Cell_____

E-mail _____

Notes _____

_____

═══

Name _____

Address _____ Apt/Unit # _____

City _____ State _____ Zip _____

Phone _____ Cell_____

E-mail _____

Notes _____

_____

═══

Name _____

Address _____ Apt/Unit # _____

City _____ State _____ Zip _____

Phone _____ Cell_____

E-mail _____

Notes _____

_____

_____

Name _____

Address _____ Apt/Unit # _____

City _____ State _____ Zip _____

Phone _____ Cell_____

E-mail _____

Notes _____

_____

Name _____

Address _____ Apt/Unit # _____

City _____ State _____ Zip _____

Phone _____ Cell_____

E-mail _____

Notes _____

_____

Name _____

Address _____ Apt/Unit # _____

City _____ State _____ Zip _____

Phone _____ Cell_____

E-mail _____

Notes _____

_____

_____

Name _____

Address _____ Apt/Unit # _____

City _____ State _____ Zip _____

Phone _____ Cell_____

E-mail _____

Notes _____

_____

Name _____

Address _____ Apt/Unit # _____

City _____ State _____ Zip _____

Phone _____ Cell_____

E-mail _____

Notes _____

_____

Name _____

Address _____ Apt/Unit # _____

City _____ State _____ Zip _____

Phone _____ Cell_____

E-mail _____

Notes _____

_____

Name _____

Address _____ Apt/Unit # _____

City _____ State _____ Zip _____

Phone _____ Cell _____

E-mail _____

Notes _____

_____

Name _____

Address _____ Apt/Unit # _____

City _____ State _____ Zip _____

Phone _____ Cell _____

E-mail _____

Notes _____

_____

Name _____

Address _____ Apt/Unit # _____

City _____ State _____ Zip _____

Phone _____ Cell _____

E-mail _____

Notes _____

_____

THE LARGEST WHALES

The largest toothed whale is the sperm whale. Reaching a length of 57 feet, their head takes up a third of their body length. They are the deepest diver of the large whales, diving down to 7300 feet, where they hunt for their main food source – squid. Whalers hunted the Sperm whale for their prized oil stored in their melon.

Everything about the blue whale is big. It is thought to be the largest animal to have ever lived, reaching up to 100 ft. It is larger than any known dinosaur. However, there is currently a long-necked dinosaur fossil being unearthed in Argentina that may surpass the blue whale. A blue whale's heart is the size of a small car. Its tongue weighs as much as an elephant. A blue whale calf drinks 100 gallons of milk a day and gains 8-10 lbs. an hour, or two hundred pounds a day. They grow at the rate of 1.5 inches a day. If a newborn human grew at this rate, it would be six feet in 6.8 weeks.

The second largest baleen whale is the fin whale. For its size, it is the fastest swimmer of the large whales, reaching speeds of 23 mph. It is often referred to as the greyhound of the ocean.

The bowhead whale may be the longest living whale. It is estimated to live around 200 years, which means if these whales have memory,

some of them could remember back to when they were hunted by whalers. It is also one of the whales that gives births to twins.

Name _____

Address _____ Apt/Unit # _____

City _____ State _____ Zip _____

Phone _____ Cell_____

E-mail _____

Notes _____

_____

Name _____

Address _____ Apt/Unit # _____

City _____ State _____ Zip _____

Phone _____ Cell_____

E-mail _____

Notes _____

_____

Name _____

Address _____ Apt/Unit # _____

City _____ State _____ Zip _____

Phone _____ Cell_____

E-mail _____

Notes _____

_____

_____

Name _____

Address _____ Apt/Unit # _____

City _____ State _____ Zip _____

Phone _____ Cell_____

E-mail _____

Notes _____

_____

Name _____

Address _____ Apt/Unit # _____

City _____ State _____ Zip _____

Phone _____ Cell_____

E-mail _____

Notes _____

_____

Name _____

Address _____ Apt/Unit # _____

City _____ State _____ Zip _____

Phone _____ Cell_____

E-mail _____

Notes _____

_____

_____

Name _____

Address _____ Apt/Unit # _____

City _____ State _____ Zip _____

Phone _____ Cell_____

E-mail _____

Notes _____

_____

═══

Name _____

Address _____ Apt/Unit # _____

City _____ State _____ Zip _____

Phone _____ Cell_____

E-mail _____

Notes _____

_____

═══

Name _____

Address _____ Apt/Unit # _____

City _____ State _____ Zip _____

Phone _____ Cell_____

E-mail _____

Notes _____

_____

_____

Name _____

Address _____ Apt/Unit # _____

City _____ State _____ Zip _____

Phone _____ Cell _____

E-mail _____

Notes _____

_____

Name _____

Address _____ Apt/Unit # _____

City _____ State _____ Zip _____

Phone _____ Cell _____

E-mail _____

Notes _____

_____

Name _____

Address _____ Apt/Unit # _____

City _____ State _____ Zip _____

Phone _____ Cell _____

E-mail _____

Notes _____

_____

_____

Name _____

Address _____ Apt/Unit # _____

City _____ State _____ Zip _____

Phone _____ Cell_____

E-mail _____

Notes _____

_____

===

Name _____

Address _____ Apt/Unit # _____

City _____ State _____ Zip _____

Phone _____ Cell_____

E-mail _____

Notes _____

_____

===

Name _____

Address _____ Apt/Unit # _____

City _____ State _____ Zip _____

Phone _____ Cell_____

E-mail _____

Notes _____

_____

_____

Name _____

Address _____ Apt/Unit # _____

City _____ State _____ Zip _____

Phone _____ Cell_____

E-mail _____

Notes _____

_____

Name _____

Address _____ Apt/Unit # _____

City _____ State _____ Zip _____

Phone _____ Cell_____

E-mail _____

Notes _____

_____

Name _____

Address _____ Apt/Unit # _____

City _____ State _____ Zip _____

Phone _____ Cell_____

E-mail _____

Notes _____

_____

Name _____

Address _____ Apt/Unit # _____

City _____ State _____ Zip _____

Phone _____ Cell_____

E-mail _____

Notes _____

_____

===

Name _____

Address _____ Apt/Unit # _____

City _____ State _____ Zip _____

Phone _____ Cell_____

E-mail _____

Notes _____

_____

===

Name _____

Address _____ Apt/Unit # _____

City _____ State _____ Zip _____

Phone _____ Cell_____

E-mail _____

Notes _____

_____

===

17. Ambergris, a whale byproduct, is used in the manufacturing of perfume. What is ambergris?

   ___ Whale urine   ___ Whale poop

   ___ Whale blubber   ___ Whale oil

18. How much milk does a blue whale calf drink a day?

   ___ Twenty gallons   ___ Fifty gallons

   ___ A hundred gallons   ___ Two hundred gallon

19. No whale eats other whales?

   ___ True   ___ False

20. Which whale is called the "Canary of the Sea"?

   ___ Beluga whale`   ___ Narwhal

   ___ Beaked whale   ___ Vaquita

21. What was the percentage of blue whales killed during the whaling years?

   ___ 99%   ___ 50%

   ___ 75%`   ___ 85%

22. How did the Right Whale gets its name?

   ___ It was not hunted by whalers

   ___ It was the "right" whale to hunt because it floated after dying, making the whalers' job earlier

   ___ It is the only prehistoric whale

   ___ It is both dolphin and whale

23. Gray whales are unique in its eating habit because?

   ___ It eats only salmon   ___ It eats other whales

   ___ Is a bottom feeder   ___ It dives into the deep ocean

Name _____

Address _____ Apt/Unit # _____

City _____ State _____ Zip _____

Phone _____ Cell_____

E-mail _____

Notes _____

_____

Name _____

Address _____ Apt/Unit # _____

City _____ State _____ Zip _____

Phone _____ Cell_____

E-mail _____

Notes _____

_____

Name _____

Address _____ Apt/Unit # _____

City _____ State _____ Zip _____

Phone _____ Cell_____

E-mail _____

Notes _____

_____

_____

Name _____

Address _____ Apt/Unit # _____

City _____ State _____ Zip _____

Phone _____ Cell_____

E-mail _____

Notes _____

_____

Name _____

Address _____ Apt/Unit # _____

City _____ State _____ Zip _____

Phone _____ Cell_____

E-mail _____

Notes _____

_____

Name _____

Address _____ Apt/Unit # _____

City _____ State _____ Zip _____

Phone _____ Cell_____

E-mail _____

Notes _____

_____

_____

Name _____

Address _____ Apt/Unit # _____

City _____ State _____ Zip _____

Phone _____ Cell_____

E-mail _____

Notes _____

_____

═══

Name _____

Address _____ Apt/Unit # _____

City _____ State _____ Zip _____

Phone _____ Cell_____

E-mail _____

Notes _____

_____

═══

Name _____

Address _____ Apt/Unit # _____

City _____ State _____ Zip _____

Phone _____ Cell_____

E-mail _____

Notes _____

_____

_____

Name _____

Address _____ Apt/Unit # _____

City _____ State _____ Zip _____

Phone _____ Cell_____

E-mail _____

Notes _____

_____

Name _____

Address _____ Apt/Unit # _____

City _____ State _____ Zip _____

Phone _____ Cell_____

E-mail _____

Notes _____

_____

Name _____

Address _____ Apt/Unit # _____

City _____ State _____ Zip _____

Phone _____ Cell_____

E-mail _____

Notes _____

_____

_____

Name _____

Address _____ Apt/Unit # _____

City _____ State _____ Zip _____

Phone _____ Cell_____

E-mail _____

Notes _____

_____

Name _____

Address _____ Apt/Unit # _____

City _____ State _____ Zip _____

Phone _____ Cell_____

E-mail _____

Notes _____

_____

Name _____

Address _____ Apt/Unit # _____

City _____ State _____ Zip _____

Phone _____ Cell_____

E-mail _____

Notes _____

_____

_____

Name _____

Address _____ Apt/Unit # _____

City _____ State _____ Zip _____

Phone _____ Cell _____

E-mail _____

Notes _____

_____

Name _____

Address _____ Apt/Unit # _____

City _____ State _____ Zip _____

Phone _____ Cell _____

E-mail _____

Notes _____

_____

Name _____

Address _____ Apt/Unit # _____

City _____ State _____ Zip _____

Phone _____ Cell _____

E-mail _____

Notes _____

_____

Name _____

Address _____ Apt/Unit # _____

City _____ State _____ Zip _____

Phone _____ Cell_____

E-mail _____

Notes _____

_____

Name _____

Address _____ Apt/Unit # _____

City _____ State _____ Zip _____

Phone _____ Cell_____

E-mail _____

Notes _____

_____

Name _____

Address _____ Apt/Unit # _____

City _____ State _____ Zip _____

Phone _____ Cell_____

E-mail _____

Notes _____

_____

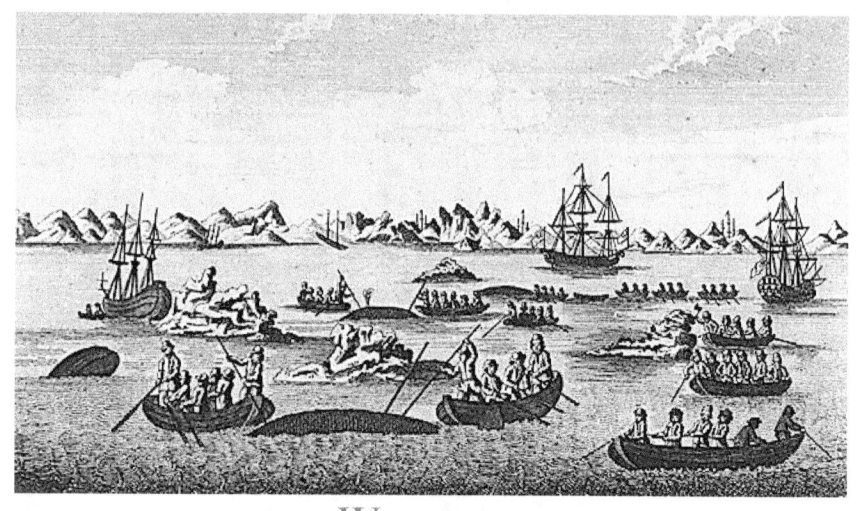

WHALING

Whaling began as far back as prehistoric times, confined mostly to coastal areas. Industrial whaling emerged with organized fleets in the 17th century, followed by competitive national whaling in the 18th and 19th century. As the demand for whale oil increased, more whales were killed. By the late 1930's, more than 50,000 whales were killed annually. Whale numbers decreased as whaling took a heavy toll on whale populations. In 1982, a morritorium on whaling was called for. Finally, in 1986, the International Whaling Commision banned commercial whaling. But the damage was already done. Many whale species were desimated. Ninety-nine percent of blue whales had been killed. The estimated 50,000 bowheads were down to 3,000.

Because of loopholes, some countries still hunt whales today. Since the ban, more than 50,000 whales have been slaughtered. Norway, Iceland and Japan take approximately 2,000 whales a year. Some aboriginal peoples are allowed to hunt a limited number of whales to meet nutritional and cultural needs.

The demand for whale meat has declined dramatically. As a result, much of the meat that is harvested is stored in huge frozen stockpiles.

Name _____

Address _____ Apt/Unit # _____

City _____ State _____ Zip _____

Phone _____ Cell_____

E-mail _____

Notes _____

_____

Name _____

Address _____ Apt/Unit # _____

City _____ State _____ Zip _____

Phone _____ Cell_____

E-mail _____

Notes _____

_____

Name _____

Address _____ Apt/Unit # _____

City _____ State _____ Zip _____

Phone _____ Cell_____

E-mail _____

Notes _____

_____

_____

Name _____

Address _____ Apt/Unit # _____

City _____ State _____ Zip _____

Phone _____ Cell_____

E-mail _____

Notes _____

_____

===

Name _____

Address _____ Apt/Unit # _____

City _____ State _____ Zip _____

Phone _____ Cell_____

E-mail _____

Notes _____

_____

===

Name _____

Address _____ Apt/Unit # _____

City _____ State _____ Zip _____

Phone _____ Cell_____

E-mail _____

Notes _____

_____

_____

Name _____

Address _____ Apt/Unit # _____

City _____ State _____ Zip _____

Phone _____ Cell_____

E-mail _____

Notes _____

_____

Name _____

Address _____ Apt/Unit # _____

City _____ State _____ Zip _____

Phone _____ Cell_____

E-mail _____

Notes _____

_____

Name _____

Address _____ Apt/Unit # _____

City _____ State _____ Zip _____

Phone _____ Cell_____

E-mail _____

Notes _____

_____

_____

Name _____

Address _____ Apt/Unit # _____

City _____ State _____ Zip _____

Phone _____ Cell _____

E-mail _____

Notes _____

_____

Name _____

Address _____ Apt/Unit # _____

City _____ State _____ Zip _____

Phone _____ Cell _____

E-mail _____

Notes _____

_____

Name _____

Address _____ Apt/Unit # _____

City _____ State _____ Zip _____

Phone _____ Cell _____

E-mail _____

Notes _____

_____

_____

Name _____

Address _____ Apt/Unit # _____

City _____ State _____ Zip _____

Phone _____ Cell _____

E-mail _____

Notes _____

_____

Name _____

Address _____ Apt/Unit # _____

City _____ State _____ Zip _____

Phone _____ Cell _____

E-mail _____

Notes _____

_____

Name _____

Address _____ Apt/Unit # _____

City _____ State _____ Zip _____

Phone _____ Cell _____

E-mail _____

Notes _____

_____

_____

Name _____

Address _____ Apt/Unit # _____

City _____ State _____ Zip _____

Phone _____ Cell_____

E-mail _____

Notes _____

_____

Name _____

Address _____ Apt/Unit # _____

City _____ State _____ Zip _____

Phone _____ Cell_____

E-mail _____

Notes _____

_____

Name _____

Address _____ Apt/Unit # _____

City _____ State _____ Zip _____

Phone _____ Cell_____

E-mail _____

Notes _____

_____

Name _____

Address _____ Apt/Unit # _____

City _____ State _____ Zip _____

Phone _____ Cell_____

E-mail _____

Notes _____

_____

Name _____

Address _____ Apt/Unit # _____

City _____ State _____ Zip _____

Phone _____ Cell_____

E-mail _____

Notes _____

_____

Name _____

Address _____ Apt/Unit # _____

City _____ State _____ Zip _____

Phone _____ Cell_____

E-mail _____

Notes _____

_____

Whale Trivia

24. Which whale lives 200 years?

____ Right whale   ____ Bowhead whale

____ Sperm whale   ____ Blue whale

25. Which dolphin that lives in Baja California will soon be extinct?

____ Vaquita   ____ Culver's beak whale

____ Risso   ____ River dolphin

26. Which whale has an elongated tooth that resembles a unicorn horn?

____ Narwhal   ____ Orca

____ Vaquita   ____ Pygmy Sperm

27. What is the difference between a porpoise and a dolphin

____ Porpoises are larger   ____ Size of the fluke

____ Shape of the teeth   ____ Location

28. The lice which lives on whales, especially Gray whales, are?

_____An insect   ____ A crustacean

____ A bacterium   ____ A fish

29. Which dolphin is the largest whale?

____ Orca   ____ Culver's beaked whale

____ Pilot whale   ____ Risso

30. What factor is impacting whale populations?

____ Global warming   ____ Reduction in fish populations

____ Warming waters   ____ Commercial ship strikes

____ All of the above   ____ Water pollution

Name _____

Address _____ Apt/Unit # _____

City _____ State _____ Zip _____

Phone _____ Cell_____

E-mail _____

Notes _____

_____

═══

Name _____

Address _____ Apt/Unit # _____

City _____ State _____ Zip _____

Phone _____ Cell_____

E-mail _____

Notes _____

_____

═══

Name _____

Address _____ Apt/Unit # _____

City _____ State _____ Zip _____

Phone _____ Cell_____

E-mail _____

Notes _____

_____

_____

Name _____

Address _____ Apt/Unit # _____

City _____ State _____ Zip _____

Phone _____ Cell _____

E-mail _____

Notes _____

_____

_____

Name _____

Address _____ Apt/Unit # _____

City _____ State _____ Zip _____

Phone _____ Cell _____

E-mail _____

Notes _____

_____

_____

Name _____

Address _____ Apt/Unit # _____

City _____ State _____ Zip _____

Phone _____ Cell _____

E-mail _____

Notes _____

_____

_____

Name _____

Address _____ Apt/Unit # _____

City _____ State _____ Zip _____

Phone _____ Cell_____

E-mail _____

Notes _____

_____

Name _____

Address _____ Apt/Unit # _____

City _____ State _____ Zip _____

Phone _____ Cell_____

E-mail _____

Notes _____

_____

Name _____

Address _____ Apt/Unit # _____

City _____ State _____ Zip _____

Phone _____ Cell_____

E-mail _____

Notes _____

_____

_____

Name _____

Address _____ Apt/Unit # _____

City _____ State _____ Zip _____

Phone _____ Cell_____

E-mail _____

Notes _____

_____

Name _____

Address _____ Apt/Unit # _____

City _____ State _____ Zip _____

Phone _____ Cell_____

E-mail _____

Notes _____

_____

Name _____

Address _____ Apt/Unit # _____

City _____ State _____ Zip _____

Phone _____ Cell_____

E-mail _____

Notes _____

_____

_____

Name _____

Address _____ Apt/Unit # _____

City _____ State _____ Zip _____

Phone _____ Cell_____

E-mail _____

Notes _____

_____

═══

Name _____

Address _____ Apt/Unit # _____

City _____ State _____ Zip _____

Phone _____ Cell_____

E-mail _____

Notes _____

_____

═══

Name _____

Address _____ Apt/Unit # _____

City _____ State _____ Zip _____

Phone _____ Cell_____

E-mail _____

Notes _____

_____

_____

Name _____

Address _____ Apt/Unit # _____

City _____ State _____ Zip _____

Phone _____ Cell_____

E-mail _____

Notes _____

_____

===

Name _____

Address _____ Apt/Unit # _____

City _____ State _____ Zip _____

Phone _____ Cell_____

E-mail _____

Notes _____

_____

===

Name _____

Address _____ Apt/Unit # _____

City _____ State _____ Zip _____

Phone _____ Cell_____

E-mail _____

Notes _____

_____

===

Name _____

Address _____ Apt/Unit # _____

City _____ State _____ Zip _____

Phone _____ Cell_____

E-mail _____

Notes _____

_____

===

Name _____

Address _____ Apt/Unit # _____

City _____ State _____ Zip _____

Phone _____ Cell_____

E-mail _____

Notes _____

_____

===

Name _____

Address _____ Apt/Unit # _____

City _____ State _____ Zip _____

Phone _____ Cell_____

E-mail _____

Notes _____

_____

===

DOLPHINS & PORPOISES

Dolphins and Porpoises are toothed whales. Although they look very much alike, there are subtle characteristics that separate these two mammals. The dolphin's dorsal fin (the one on its back) is curved or hooked, while the porpoise's dorsal fin is more of a triangle. The dolphin is longer and leaner, while the porpoise is portly. The dolphin's mouth ends in some form of a beak. Porpoises do not possess beaks. Dolphins are also more talkative and are known to engage in sex for reasons other than procreation. Both species possess melons located at the front of their foreheads, but the porpoise's is not distinguishable. Both use echolocation to catch their food.

The true test of to determine if an animal is a dolphin or porpoise is its teeth. Dolphins have conical, pointed teeth, while porpoise teeth are flatter and shaped like a spade.

There are 6 species of porpoise and 32 species of dolphin.

REMEMBER: All dolphins & porpoises are whales, but not all whales are dolphins or porpoises.

.

Name _____

Address _____ Apt/Unit # _____

City _____ State _____ Zip _____

Phone _____ Cell_____

E-mail _____

Notes _____

_____

Name _____

Address _____ Apt/Unit # _____

City _____ State _____ Zip _____

Phone _____ Cell_____

E-mail _____

Notes _____

_____

Name _____

Address _____ Apt/Unit # _____

City _____ State _____ Zip _____

Phone _____ Cell_____

E-mail _____

Notes _____

_____

_____

Name _____

Address _____ Apt/Unit # _____

City _____ State _____ Zip _____

Phone _____ Cell _____

E-mail _____

Notes _____

_____

Name _____

Address _____ Apt/Unit # _____

City _____ State _____ Zip _____

Phone _____ Cell _____

E-mail _____

Notes _____

_____

Name _____

Address _____ Apt/Unit # _____

City _____ State _____ Zip _____

Phone _____ Cell _____

E-mail _____

Notes _____

_____

_____

Name _____

Address _____ Apt/Unit # _____

City _____ State _____ Zip _____

Phone _____ Cell_____

E-mail _____

Notes _____

_____

Name _____

Address _____ Apt/Unit # _____

City _____ State _____ Zip _____

Phone _____ Cell_____

E-mail _____

Notes _____

_____

Name _____

Address _____ Apt/Unit # _____

City _____ State _____ Zip _____

Phone _____ Cell_____

E-mail _____

Notes _____

_____

_____

Name _____

Address _____ Apt/Unit # _____

City _____ State _____ Zip _____

Phone _____ Cell_____

E-mail _____

Notes _____

_____

Name _____

Address _____ Apt/Unit # _____

City _____ State _____ Zip _____

Phone _____ Cell_____

E-mail _____

Notes _____

_____

Name _____

Address _____ Apt/Unit # _____

City _____ State _____ Zip _____

Phone _____ Cell_____

E-mail _____

Notes _____

_____

_____

Name _____

Address _____ Apt/Unit # _____

City _____ State _____ Zip _____

Phone _____ Cell_____

E-mail _____

Notes _____

_____

Name _____

Address _____ Apt/Unit # _____

City _____ State _____ Zip _____

Phone _____ Cell_____

E-mail _____

Notes _____

_____

Name _____

Address _____ Apt/Unit # _____

City _____ State _____ Zip _____

Phone _____ Cell_____

E-mail _____

Notes _____

_____

_____

Name _____

Address _____ Apt/Unit # _____

City _____ State _____ Zip _____

Phone _____ Cell_____

E-mail _____

Notes _____

_____

Name _____

Address _____ Apt/Unit # _____

City _____ State _____ Zip _____

Phone _____ Cell_____

E-mail _____

Notes _____

_____

Name _____

Address _____ Apt/Unit # _____

City _____ State _____ Zip _____

Phone _____ Cell_____

E-mail _____

Notes _____

_____

Name _____

Address _____ Apt/Unit # _____

City _____ State _____ Zip _____

Phone _____ Cell_____

E-mail _____

Notes _____

_____

Name _____

Address _____ Apt/Unit # _____

City _____ State _____ Zip _____

Phone _____ Cell_____

E-mail _____

Notes _____

_____

Name _____

Address _____ Apt/Unit # _____

City _____ State _____ Zip _____

Phone _____ Cell_____

E-mail _____

Notes _____

_____

THE ENDANGERED VAQUITA

The small vaquita of Baja California is one of the most endangered whales on Earth. In 1997, the estimated number was 567. In 2014, that number dropped to 100 individuals. A new survey released in May, 2016 stated the small porpoise' population was less than 60, a decline of 92% from the 1997 estimate. At this rate, the vaquita will be extinct in the next few years.

The vaquita is being exterminated as a product of bycatch. It is drowning in the illegal gill nets used to catch a fish called the totoaba. This fish's swim bladder is highly prized as a traditional health food and medicine in China. One totoaba swim bladder is valued at roughly $5,000 on the black market in the United States, and sometimes more than $10,000 in Asian markets. A bowl of totoaba fish bladder soup in China may cost as much as $25,000. Few fishermen can resist the temptation of such money. Although Mexico has banned the gill nets, they are still being used.

The vaquita lives nowhere else in the world except in Baja. It has no close living relatives and is an evolutionarily distinct animal. It is classified as one of the top 100 evolutionary distinct and globally

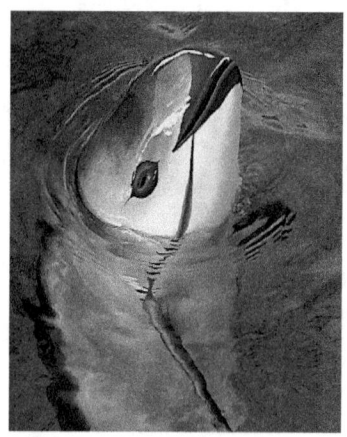

endangered (EDGE) animals in the world. Besides being listed as endangered under the Endangered Species Act, it is also listed by the IUCN and the CITES in the category of most critical risk of extinction.

The vaquita is distinguished by the dark circle around its eyes and its dark lips, often giving it the appearance of smiling. There is also a dark line that extends from its mouth to its dorsal fin.

Name _____

Address _____ Apt/Unit # _____

City _____ State _____ Zip _____

Phone _____ Cell_____

E-mail _____

Notes _____

_____

Name _____

Address _____ Apt/Unit # _____

City _____ State _____ Zip _____

Phone _____ Cell_____

E-mail _____

Notes _____

_____

Name _____

Address _____ Apt/Unit # _____

City _____ State _____ Zip _____

Phone _____ Cell_____

E-mail _____

Notes _____

_____

_____

Name _____

Address _____ Apt/Unit # _____

City _____ State _____ Zip _____

Phone _____ Cell_____

E-mail _____

Notes _____

_____

Name _____

Address _____ Apt/Unit # _____

City _____ State _____ Zip _____

Phone _____ Cell_____

E-mail _____

Notes _____

_____

Name _____

Address _____ Apt/Unit # _____

City _____ State _____ Zip _____

Phone _____ Cell_____

E-mail _____

Notes _____

_____

_____

Name _____

Address _____ Apt/Unit # _____

City _____ State _____ Zip _____

Phone _____ Cell_____

E-mail _____

Notes _____

_____

Name _____

Address _____ Apt/Unit # _____

City _____ State _____ Zip _____

Phone _____ Cell_____

E-mail _____

Notes _____

_____

Name _____

Address _____ Apt/Unit # _____

City _____ State _____ Zip _____

Phone _____ Cell_____

E-mail _____

Notes _____

_____

WHALE TRIVIA

31. Which whale has the heaviest brain?

    ___ Blue whale   ___ Sei whale

    ___ Sperm whale   ___ Fin whale

32. How fast has a bull orca been clocked swimming?

    ___ 34 mph   ___ 22 mph

    ___ 50 mph   ___ 10 mph

33. Do whales sleep?

    ___ Yes   ___ No

34. How long is a bowhead's baleen?

    ___ 20 ft.   ___ 15 ft.

    ___ 10 ft.   ___ 6 ft.

35. In a gray whale's lifetime, what is her yearly migration equivalent to?

    ___ A trip around the Earth 10 times   ___ A journey to Mars

    ___ A trip to the moon   ___ A trip to the sun

36. Which whale has the longest and most complex song?

    ___ Bryde's whale   ___ Orca

    ___ Humpback whale   ___ Bowhead whale

37. Once common in the Atlantic Ocean, the Gray whale only remains in the Pacific Ocean?

    ___ True   ___ False

38. Which whale is the deepest diver?

    ___ Sperm whale   ___ Blue whale

    ___ Cuvier's beaked whale   ___ Minke whale

NOTES

NOTES

NOTES

_____

_____

_____

_____

_____

_____

_____

_____

_____

_____

_____

_____

_____

_____

_____

_____

WHALE TRIVIA ANSWERS

1. How many nostrils does a toothed whale have?   One

2. What is baleen like?   All the above

3. How many chambers does a whale's heart have?   Four

4. What is the largest animal to have ever lived?   Blue whale

5. Which whale has the longest migration?   Gray whale

6. Do whales have hind limbs (legs)?   Yes. The hind limbs have been
     reduced to a vestigial pair of bones that represent the pelvic girdle

7. Where do deep diving whales store their oxygen?   Muscles

8. All whales locate food by sonar or echolocation.   False. Only
     toothed whales use sonar.

9. Do whales have ears?   Yes

10. All dolphins are whales.   True

11. Which toothed whale also eats marine mammals?   Orca

12. What is a whale?   A mammal

13. The whale's ancestor as a land creature who walked on all four leg.   True

14. What was the nick name given to Gray whales by whalers?   Devil Fish

15. How large is a blue whale's heart?   All the above

16. A porpoise and a dolphin are the same mammal.   False

17. What is ambergris?   Whale poop

18. How much milk does a blue whale calf drink a day?   A hundred gallons

19. No whale eats other whales.   False

20. Which whale is called the "Canary of the Sea"?   Beluga whale

21. What was the percentage of blue whales killed during the whaling years? 99%

22. How did the Right whale get its name?   It was the "right" whale to hunt
     because it floated after dying, making the whalers' job earlier

23. Gray whales are unique in its eating habit because?   Is a bottom feeder

86

24. Which whale lives 200 years   Bowhead whale

25. Which dolphin that lives in Baja California will soon be extinct?   Vaquita

26. Which whale has an elongated tooth that resembles a unicorn horn?   Narwhal

27. What is the difference between a porpoise and a dolphin?   Shape of the teeth.

   A dolphin's teeth are conical and a porpoises are spade shaped.

28. The lice which lives on whales, especially Gray whales, is?   A crustacean

29. Which dolphin is the largest whale?   Orca

30. What factor is impacting whale populations?   All of the above

31. Which whale has the heaviest brain?   Blue whale

32. How fast has a bull orca been clocked swimming?   34 mph

33. Do whales sleep?   Yes and No. They sleep, but not like us. Whales are
     voluntary breathers. Half of their brain must stay awake so the whale will
     rise to the surface and breathe.

34. How long is a bowhead's baleen?   15 ft.

35. In a gray whale's lifetime, what is her yearly migration equivalent to?
                                                          A trip to the moon
36. Which whale has the longest and most complex song?   Humpback whale

37. Once common in the Atlantic Ocean, the Gray whale only remains in the
Pacific Ocean?   True. The Gray whale was wiped out of the Atlantic
     approximately 200 years ago. It is believed to be the result of over hunting
     and natural causes.

38. Which whale is the deepest diver?   Cuvier's beaked whale
     is estimated to dive as deep as 9800 ft. A sperm whale, once thought to be the
     deepest diving whale, dives to an estimated 7200 ft.

SHE WAS NEVER MEANT TO BE HUMAN!

The Europa Saga

A tale of suspense, adventure, assassins, survival and truth. Start the adventure today.

Get book one, EUROPA Awakenings, for free at
https://www.smashwords.com/books/view/633078

http://www.prgarcia1.com

JOURNALS DESIGNED BY
P. R. Garcia

Christmas Address Book
with Christmas Trivia

Christmas Address Book
with Christmas Traditions

Whale Daily Journal

Companion for SciFi writer

Available on Amazon or at http://www.prgarcia1.com – the journal page.